W9-BLD-253

PRESENTED TO

_____

FROM

_____

DATE

_____

Journey to Bethlehem

An Advent Collection

ARNOLD R. FLEAGLE

with calligraphy by TIMOTHY R. BOTTS

Christian Publications
Camp Hill, Pennsylvania

Christian Publications
3825 Hartzdale Drive
Camp Hill, PA 17011

Faithful, biblical publishing since 1883

ISBN: 0-87509-637-9
LOC Catalog Card Number: 96-84250

96 97 98 99 00   5 4 3 2 1

Unless otherwise noted, poetry written by the author.

To Matthew and Marc, my two sons,

who have made the Journey to Bethlehem

each year since their advents in 1981 and 1983

CONTENTS

PREFACE

Journey to Bethlehem is a Christmas reader designed for a general audience. My hope is that it will serve as a devotional roadmap through the colors and characters, the places and prophecies, the songs and sights of Christmas. My prime objective is to enrich the understanding of those who travel through its pages with the visible picture of the invisible God, Jesus Christ. Christmas, in its most noble sense, is the worship of the Messiah who was born into a tiny manger.

My expectations for this book have been escalated by the calligraphy of Timothy Botts, a man who pursues the holiness of God and whose unique gift has illuminated the path to Him.

My highest prayer is that the Holy Spirit will go beyond human preparation and enable the user to integrate the virtues and values that emerge from this great drama which marks the intersection of earth and heaven, time and eternity, humanity and deity.

ACKNOWLEDGMENTS

My gratitude is extended to those who assisted
in the typing of the manuscript, including
Jeanne Berry, Jeanne Brenneman, Marie Hauptman,
Ann Madeira and Liz Umholtz.
The contributions of David Fessenden,
my friend and the editor
for this special project, were significant.
Kerry Hoke should be recognized for her
valuable editorial touches to the text.

Back to Bethlehem

So Joseph also went up from the town of Nazareth in Galilee
to Judea, to Bethlehem the town of David,
because he belonged to the house and line of David.

LUKE 2:4

*B*ETHLEHEM was a tiny town a few miles south of the Holy City, Jerusalem. Though meager in demographics, its impact on biblical history is substantial. Bethlehem was the burial ground of Rachel, the beloved wife of Jacob. In Bethlehem, the mighty David was born and as he grew to manhood, Samuel chose to anoint him as king in the village of his birth. But it was the prophecy of Micah spoken seven centuries before the birth of the Messiah that stirred the imagination and precipitated impatience among the Jewish people who earnestly longed for their Deliverer. The ancient prophet forecast:

> *But you, Bethlehem Ephrathah, though you are small among the clans of Judah,*
> *out of you will come for me one who will be ruler over Israel,*
> *whose origins are from of old, from ancient times. (Micah 5:2)*

NOVEMBER
24

The Heavenly Father had designed another "coincidence" in the panoramic plan of salvation. This seemingly insignificant town would be the cradle of His answer to man's sinful existence. Bethlehem, which means "house of bread," would provide the birthplace for "The Bread of Life."

How would the awesome God orchestrate the fulfillment of this ancient prediction? It is fascinating that God would use taxation to guide Joseph, a descendant of David, and Mary, his expectant wife, to this particular place. Caesar's decree directed this couple to the exact location that Micah had foretold. It is within God's sovereignty to utilize methods and means, places and personnel that you and I would never consider in order to accomplish His grand plan!

God employed the angelic choir to direct the shepherds to the city of David. Despite their duty to watch sheep, they went back to Bethlehem, for after the departure of the angels they collectively agreed, "Let's go to Bethlehem and see this thing that has happened, which the Lord has told us about" (Luke 2:15). Their work did not suffocate their passionate desire to see the Savior.

Let's go back to Bethlehem this Christmas!

However, there is one group who knew where Jesus was to be born, but who never searched for Him! When Herod inquired of the chief priests and scribes where the King of the Jews was to be born, they answered correctly, "In Bethlehem in Judea" (Matthew 2:5). But neither Herod nor his advisors ran to probe the place of the Messiah's birth. Herod and these religious leaders sent the magi to discover the Deliverer's whereabouts, rather than going themselves. They knew about Bethlehem. It was so nearby. Yet they never witnessed Jesus Christ "up close and personal."

Will you go back to Bethlehem this Christmas? Will you imitate the shepherds and make time to worship the Savior? Or will you know about

Him and where to encounter Him, but somehow not be committed to finding a way to Bethlehem? He awaits your presence at His birthday celebration! Let's go to Bethlehem!

BACK TO BETHLEHEM

Back to Bethlehem, Let me see,
A special gift sent for me;
Heaven's priceless child from above,
Jesus Christ the Lamb of Love.

Back to Bethlehem, Let me stay,
By His manger bed where He lay;
The Holy One from above,
Jesus Christ the Lamb of Love.

DEAR MIGHTY GOD, *like Bethlehem, I am small and insignificant. Stretch my faith and use my gifts so that, like Bethlehem, I may be of significance to You.*

THE PROMISE

But when the time had fully come, God sent his Son,
born of a woman, born under law, to redeem those under law,
that we might receive the full rights of sons.

GALATIANS 4:4-5

*T*HE church leader of an evangelical denomination was being badgered at a general conference about a sticky problem which had no kindergarten solution. He finally vented his frustration with this remark, "If my foresight were as good as my hindsight, I'd be out of sight."

The incarnation of Christ at Christmas is the answer of the ages to the sticky problem of sin and its far-reaching ramifications. It was long-predicted, but just as long in coming.

As we contemplate the Jewish people and their expectations of a Messiah, we are reminded by history of the extended duration of their vigil. Five empires, Assyria, Babylonia, Persia, Greece and Rome had exercised dominion over them. They were detained, dismantled, discouraged and disappointed. Nevertheless, some of God's people still clung to the hope that David's heir would one special day make His appearance to deliver His descendants.

A road sign in Pennsylvania reads, "Antiques made while you wait." What a reflection of the mindset of impatient disciples in an "instant coffee" age! We must learn the lesson of God's patient and panoramic plan. For, when God acts, that moment can redirect the rivers of our history.

NOVEMBER
25

Dennis Kinlaw, President of Asbury College, exclaimed, "Give me one divine moment when God acts and that is greater than all the works of men throughout the centuries!"

The Christmas message, delivered in a tiny manger, broadcasts loudly that God remembers His promises! It is time to reclaim our heritage and hope. It is time to renew our prayers and practices regarding the great goals in our lives. It is time to remember that "He has made everything beautiful in its time" (Ecclesiastes 3:11). What you and I may have wanted yesterday, God may desire today or tomorrow.

God is faithful to remember His promises!

The desperate author who wrote his publisher with a passionate plea for money stated the question: "How much advance will you pay me for my 50,000-word manuscript?" The publisher replied with another question, "How important are the words?"

Galatians 4:4 possesses a monumental phrase with an incalculable value for the twentieth-century Christian: "But when the time had fully come . . ." May the stockings of our foresight be filled with faith as we consider a promise remembered.

O COME, O COME EMMANUEL

O come, O come, Emmanuel,
And ransom captive Israel,
That mourns in lonely exile here
Until the Son of God appear.

Rejoice! Rejoice!
Emmanuel Shall come to thee, O Israel!

Latin hymn

HEAVENLY FATHER, *help me to remember that You are never too early or too late. Enable me to look beyond my watch and to trust Your faithfulness to fulfill what You have promised.*

Therefore the Lord himself will give you a sign:
The virgin will be with child and will give birth to a son,
and will call him Immanuel.

ISAIAH 7:14

SHAKESPEARE in Romeo and Juliet included these classic words, "What's in a name? That which we call a rose by any other name would smell as sweet." The implication is simple: Names aren't very important! However, to the student of the Bible, names are critical, and without a deep understanding of them biblical theology becomes rather shallow. The Lord God Almighty has a fascination with names and often plays upon them to get His point across.

The first occurrence of the name *Immanuel* in the inspired Word is discovered in the shaky soil of Israel's history when the nation is threatened by Syria and Samaria. God speaks to King Ahaz by way of Isaiah the prophet, "Behold, a virgin shall conceive, and bear a son, and shall call his name Immanuel" (7:14, KJV). The Hebrew meaning, "God is with us," was attached to the miraculous birth. The name of the baby, each time it was mentioned, brought peace to a troubled monarch's soul.

In the first chapter of the New Testament, after 700 years of captivity in the hands of man and 400 years of prophetic silence, an angel steps into the dream of a carpenter. The angel assures him that the virgin Mary is with child of the Holy Spirit and that the endangered marriage

NOVEMBER
26

must be carried out! Since it was customary for the Jewish father to name the child, the angel supplies his choice—Jesus! Then the writer of the gospel adds,

> All this took place to fulfill what the Lord had said through the prophet:
> "The virgin will be with child and will give birth to a son, and they will call
> him Immanuel"—which means, "God with us." (Matthew 1:22-23)

Immanuel means I am never alone!

Immanuel means everything to the believer! Because of Immanuel, the fiery furnace became a fortress of faith for the three Hebrew children! The lion's den became a private prayer chamber for Daniel because of Immanuel. The infested environments of modern missionaries became sacred shrines because of Immanuel. The unemployment line, the intensive care unit, the funeral parlor—all are hallowed ground because of Immanuel. It doesn't matter where you stand or what ecstasy or agony you face; it only matters who is with you!

O LITTLE TOWN OF BETHLEHEM

O Holy Child of Bethlehem!
Descend to us, we pray;
Cast out our sin, and enter in,
Be born in us today.
We hear the Christmas angels
The great glad tidings tell;
Oh, come to us, abide with us,
Our Lord Emmanuel.

Phillips Brooks

THANK YOU,
HEAVENLY
FATHER,
for Your
immanence. Thank
You for sending
Immanuel,
Jesus Christ, to
dwell on this
planet among
people like me.
Thank You for
Your Holy Spirit
who has taken His
residence in the
castle of my heart.

a teenager in Nazareth

But the angel said to her,
"Do not be afraid, Mary, you have found favor with God."

LUKE 1:30

THE characters of Christmas present the reader with a most unusual assortment of people. If you evaluate God's choices for the cast of history's most spectacular birth, you probably will be somewhat puzzled. The characters of the first Christmas not only surprise us, but they also encourage us. Their humanity, their ordinary lifestyles, their reluctance, their paralysis as they encounter angels, their synthetic solutions, all of these realities and more open the door for our own participation in the great drama that the Heavenly Father is conducting through the time line of human history.

Mary is a distinct example of heavenly typecasting. By modern standards, the mother who would carry and bear Deity wrapped in human flesh would have been a power broker, a person with money and clout, a lady who turned heads because of her sophistication and wealth, a woman who possessed all this world's desirables. But God had a different and daring idea.

NOVEMBER
27

He chose for this once-in-an-eternity part a teenager from a disreputable city named Nazareth, a young woman who had neither married nor been a mother before. Age, hometown, marital status and maternal experience, all of these disqualified her. Yet, God selected her for history's most coveted female role: mother of the Holy One of God, Jesus Christ.

What attracted history's Choreographer to this young, poor, single maiden? What made her the leading lady in the greatest story ever told? What distinguished her from all the women who walked the planet in that period of history? The highly touted angel, Gabriel, provides the answer. He introduces himself with this short assessment, "Greetings, you who are highly favored! The Lord is with you" (Luke 1:28). She had been honored with favored status. Upon hearing the accolade, she reacts with fear. The angel reassures her by rephrasing the tribute: "Mary, you have found favor with God" (1:30).

She was only a teenager in Nazareth!

The word for favor in the original Greek is the same word that is used for the word grace. This teenager in Nazareth was selected on the basis of her internal character, the appearance of her soul. The all-seeing God looks deep inside when He picks a player for His team. When the Lord spoke to Samuel about Saul's disqualification as King of Israel, He emphasized that the heart is the defining factor. "Do not consider his appearance or his height, for I have rejected him. The LORD does not look at the things man looks at. Man looks at the outward appearance, but the LORD looks at the heart" (1 Samuel 16:7).

As we long to celebrate the birth of Christ this Christmas season, it is imperative that we focus on our motivations for giving and the condition of our heart which cradles the very Spirit of Jesus Christ. God's drama continues to be acted out on the platform of human history. If you want to be chosen by Him, you must acquire most favored status. Be a person of grace, not a person wearied and worn, pressed and stressed by the panic of all that surrounds the birthday of the King.

Prepare your heart to cradle the incomparable beauty of Jesus Christ this Christmas. Perhaps all future generations will not call you blessed (Luke 1:48), but maybe, just maybe, this generation will praise God that you are favored, a person of grace, who brought Jesus to your time and people. Mary had little to attract the world's attention, but she had the one qualification that attracted God's attention, a holy heart!

THE MAGNIFICAT (One of Luke's Four Christmas Hymns)

And Mary said: "My soul glorifies the Lord and my spirit rejoices in God my Savior, for he has been mindful of the humble state of his servant. From now on all generations will call me blessed, for the Mighty One has done great things for me—holy is his name. His mercy extends to those who fear him, from generation to generation. He has performed mighty deeds with his arm; he has scattered those who are proud in their inmost thoughts. He has brought down rulers from their thrones but has lifted up the humble. He has filled the hungry with good things but has sent the rich away empty. He has helped his servant Israel, remembering to be merciful to Abraham and his descendants forever, even as he said to our fathers." (Luke 1:46-55)

DEAR LORD,

I want to be chosen this Christmas to act out the drama of Jesus Christ in me. Don't allow me to disqualify myself because of outward appearances or circumstances. I ask that Your workmanship might be evident in me as I interact with family and friends. Empower me to make the invisible Christ visible.

The Dreamer

But after he had considered this, an angel of the Lord
appeared to him in a dream and said,
"Joseph son of David, do not be afraid
to take Mary home as your wife,
because what is conceived in her is from the Holy Spirit."

MATTHEW 1:20

*F*IVE times the phrase "in a dream" appears in the first two chapters of Matthew's Gospel. Four times the phrase applies to the foster father of Jesus, Joseph of Nazareth. The only exception is in reference to the wise men who "having been warned in a dream not to go back to Herod, they returned to their country by another route" (Matthew 2:12).

The dreams of Joseph are a fascinating component of the Christmas story. The sovereign God utilized a unique mode of revelation to communicate to Joseph His preferred will. Joseph's first dream directed him to marry his fiancée Mary, who was with child (1:20). Because of her presumed guilt in having intimacy outside of her engagement, she was liable to a violent death. Joseph had previously determined that Mary would not be stoned to death, but rather he would divorce her quietly. However, the initial dream revealed that her pregnancy was arranged by the Holy Spirit.

The flight to Egypt was triggered by the second dream (2:13). The wise men had not only invited Herod's interest in the baby Jesus, they had escalated his insecurity, and he delivered a decree that all male babies in Bethlehem and its hinterlands would be slaughtered. Joseph's itinerary led him south into Egypt to escape the king's painful paranoia.

NOVEMBER
28

The third dream informed Joseph of Herod's death (2:19-20). The family was then invited to head North into Palestine. Joseph's fourth dream (2:22-23) was necessary because Herod's son, Archelaus, was the "new sheriff" in Judea. This disclosure not only removed the child Jesus from danger, it repositioned Mary and Joseph in their hometown of Nazareth fulfilling the prophesy, "and he went and lived in a town called Nazareth. So was fulfilled what was said through the prophets: `He will be called a Nazarene' " (2:23).

God speaks in a variety of ways!

The responsive obedience of Joseph is a testimonial to the righteous posture of the man. God said it, he believed it and that was sufficient. There are no debates recorded in the narration to indicate that Joseph balked or questioned the game plan. God was the coach; he was the quarterback. And when the coach called a play, the quarterback did not execute a different one.

Joseph is labeled the "forgotten man of Christmas." This couple from Nazareth had one Academy Award winner and one Best Supporting Actor. Mary is most revered and remembered, while Joseph is almost a footnote in the Christmas music and manuscript. I found twenty-three Christmas hymns in one denominational hymnal and only one of them mentioned Joseph.

Perhaps the task God assigns us is not the most visible. Maybe God will place us "behind the scenes." There may be no trophies or medals, no accolades or affirmations. We are called to do it regardless of earthly fanfare or the lack of it. Like Joseph we must listen to His voice. Joseph could have listened to his ego and not married a pregnant woman. He could have shunned all the responsibility of a baby that was not conceived by him. He could have objected to the southern and northern journeys he was called to make in order to accomplish God's plan. However, he decided to exhibit, as Nietzsche stated, "a long obedience in the same direction."

ARISE, THE KINGDOM IS AT HAND

Arise, the kingdom is at hand,
The King is drawing nigh;
Arise with joy, thou faithful band,
To meet the Lord most high!
Look up, ye souls weighed down with care,
The sovereign is not far;
Look up, faint hearts, from your despair,
Behold, the Morning Star!

Johann Rist

DEAR FATHER, *May my ears discern Your voice, and may I resolve to do Your will in my heart. I aspire that Joseph's obedient legacy be imitated by my own life.*

The people living in darkness have seen a great light;
on those living in the land of the shadow of death
a light has dawned.

MATTHEW 4:16

*I*T is one of the best attended evening services of the year. The Christmas Eve Candlelight Service is a favorite worship experience for millions in Christendom. The climax of this event is the shrouding of the sanctuary in darkness. Then, from one solitary candle, "the Christ Candle," light is passed to the pastor, then to the ushers and finally to the expectant congregation. A single light shines in the darkness, symbolizing Jesus Christ, and from that light comes a multitude of other lights which dismiss the darkness and reveal the world around us. Matthew 4:16 vividly illustrates the impact of the Light. "The people living in darkness have seen a great light; on those living in the land of the shadow of death a light has dawned."

NOVEMBER
29

This verse is a quotation from Isaiah 9:1-2 which prophesied 700 years before Jesus' birth that a light would shine in Northern Palestine around the Sea of Galilee. Zebulun and Naphtali are two of the twelve tribes and their domains are at the 11 o'clock and 12 o'clock positions in the Holy Land. Isaiah 9 is also the chapter in which the birth of a son to a virgin is foretold. So the explosion of light in the region of Galilee and the coming of Christ the Messiah are coupled together in this chapter. This may serve to reinforce that Christmas is a proper time to re-member that God came to earth with an incredible burst of light.

The word for light in the original language of the New Testament is *phos* which in English is the basis for our word photography, or "light writing." The amazing thing is that Jesus not only applied the word to Himself, but to all of His followers as well. Matthew 5:14-16 sets the pace for us this Christmas season for it details our purpose to be lights for Him:

> *You are the light of the world. A city on a hill cannot be hidden. Neither do people light a lamp and put it under a bowl. Instead they put it on its stand, and it gives light to everyone in the house. In the same way, let your light shine before men, that they may see your good deeds and praise your Father in heaven.*

One candle makes a difference in a dark room!

It is true that every good deed done in Jesus' name is another ray of light dispersed into the deep darkness, illuminating the room, the neighborhood, the hospital ward, the gymnasium, the office, the delivery truck, wherever you are. Any place where darkness dwells, you and I are assigned to tackle it. Paul's words to the Ephesians still ring with truth: "For you were once darkness, but now you are light in the Lord. Live as children of light" (5:8).

THE PEOPLE THAT IN DARKNESS SAT

The people that in darkness sat
A glorious Light have seen.
The Light has shined on them who long
In shades of night have been.

John Morison

DEAR
FATHER,
wash the windows
of my heart so that
the light of Jesus
Christ may shine
through me
without
obstruction. I am
only one candle,
but I am willing to
dispel darkness.
Place me where I
may make a
difference this
advent season.

INFINITE
BECOMES
intimate

And being found in appearance as a man, he humbled himself and became obedient to death—even death on a cross! Therefore God exalted him to the highest place and gave him the name that is above every name, that at the name of Jesus every knee should bow, in heaven and on earth and under the earth, and every tongue confess that Jesus Christ is Lord, to the glory of God the Father.

PHILIPPIANS 2:8-11

*T*HE identity of the individual has been suppressed in the twentieth century. You and I are now cataloged by numbers, symbols and computer chips. This same loss of identity can be found within the church as well. One of the most effective arguments against organized religion is the aloofness and distance which exists between leadership and laity. A great gulf has been established which very few venture across. Christianity, an extension of Judaism, has eliminated this obstacle with an up-close and personal encounter.

Isaiah's prophesies alluded to the Messiah's visit as being personal when he projected, "unto us a child is born, unto us a son is given" (9:6, KJV). Whereas the Old Testament said "unto us," the angel said "unto you" (Luke 2:11, KJV). The infinite God has become intimate. We are the primary targets of God's grace and God's glory. He took a personal interest in our dilemma and in our destiny by becoming incarnate so that we might become immortal.

Think about the accessibility which He provided through this beautiful Christmas story. Think about the baby in Bethlehem packaging Himself in our humanity and temporarily laying aside His divinity. This was an in-

NOVEMBER
30

credible sacrifice for God, the preeminent One. Our ancestors saw Him with their eyes, heard Him with their ears, spoke to Him with their lips, smelled Him with their nostrils, felt Him with their hands. Indeed Immanuel, God, has come to dwell among us and to make a difference for you and me! Heaven is not interested in bureaucracy but rather blessings and atonement for you!

A little girl climbed up upon her mother's knee and said, "Mommy, tell me a story of Jesus and put me in it!" All of us are included in this most marvelous drama we call Christmas and in the most miraculous enterprise we call the kingdom of God. There are no exemptions, for the Christmas story embraces every man and woman that has lived, is living or will ever live. God downsized Himself to the confines of mankind to love us as no other is capable. In the carol "Joy to the World" we sing: "He comes to make His blessings flow, Far as the curse is found."

Yes, this One from heaven who was placed into Mary's womb is committed to everyone who needs a Savior and a Lord.

Jesus humbled Himself so that others might be exalted!

O COME ALL YE FAITHFUL

O come, all ye faithful, Joyful and triumphant,
O come ye, O come ye to Bethlehem;
Come and behold Him Born the King of angels.
O come, let us adore Him, O come, let us adore Him,
O come, let us adore Him, Christ the Lord.

Latin hymn

DEAR FATHER, *I am humbled and honored by the incarnation of Jesus Christ. His coming as a man teaches me about the priority of placing others before myself. May this Christmas find me addressing the needs of those less fortunate than me.*

First Love

We love because he first loved us.

1 JOHN 4:19

A HOLIDAY cantata features a song entitled, "Love Came Down at Christmas." Someone has defined love in these terms: "Love is making your problem my problem." God has been reaching out to mankind with expressions of love since the beginning of human history. After the fall of Adam and Eve, He deals with their nakedness by clothing them with the skin of animals (Genesis 3:21). He preserves a remnant of the race, in the person of Noah and seven other family members, to repopulate the earth after the monstrous flood. He chooses the nation of Israel to spread the gracious and loving message of redemption.

And Christmas personified God's love as Jesus Christ was conceived in Mary's womb by the Holy Spirit. The incarnation, the downsizing of deity into the dimension of time and space, was the price of first love. The limitations of the human experience were strapped to the King of kings and the Lord of lords. The mighty Messiah was found in a manger in the tiny, insignificant town of Bethlehem.

DECEMBER
1

Christmas is the story of God becoming man so that the sons of men could become the sons of God. The Heavenly Father initiated first love in order to restore His relationship with fallen man. The birth of Jesus Christ is the tangible beginning of the New Covenant which God established with humanity.

First love is the challenge of Christmas. God took the initiative with His love that first Christmas season, and His children should imitate that first love. You can exercise first love by extending a hand to someone who has wronged you or by speaking first to that family member who has ignored you. You can be the first one to admit your fault in a dispute or the first one to ask for forgiveness.

If you can offer first love you will be amazed by the results. Be the first to love this Advent season! The heavenly Father did not cross us off His Christmas list, He didn't throw up His holy hands in disgust and He didn't forsake us. He gave us first love wrapped in the womb of a girl from Nazareth.

God's love took the initiative!

Romans 5:8 highlights the personality of God, "But God demonstrates his own love for us in this: While we were still sinners, Christ died for us." And Jesus challenges us in the same way with His command in Luke 6:35: "But love your enemies, do good to them, and lend to them without expecting to get anything back. Then your reward will be great, and you will be sons of the Most High, because he is kind to the ungrateful and wicked." As children of the Father we are called to imitate His lifestyle of first love. Who will receive first love from you this day?

SILENT NIGHT! HOLY NIGHT!

Silent night! Holy night!
Son of God, love's pure light,
Radiant beams from Thy holy face,
With the dawn of redeeming grace,
Jesus, Lord, at Thy birth,
Jesus, Lord and Thy birth.

Joseph Mohr

DEAR FATHER, *I am drawn to You because of the first love which You have tendered to me. Use me as a channel this Christmas season that I might touch those who are in need of Your first love.*

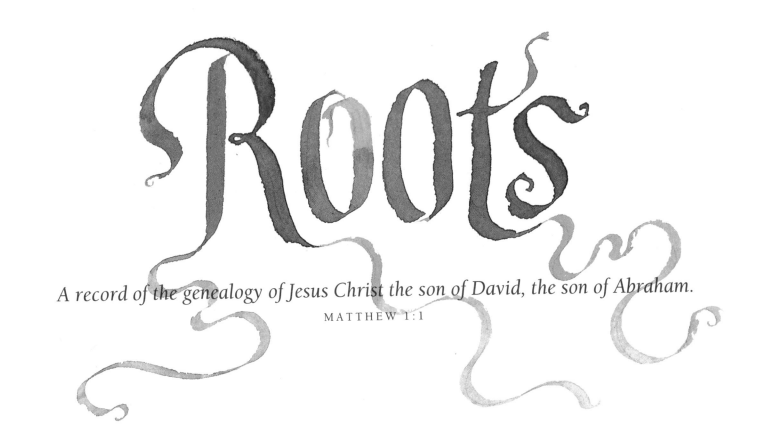

Roots

A record of the genealogy of Jesus Christ the son of David, the son of Abraham.

MATTHEW 1:1

*A*LEX HALEY wrote a best-selling book entitled *Roots*. It traced the ancestry of a black slave boy back to his distant ancestor, Kunta Kinta. The story on television was a smashing success, for it appealed to the sense of history in all of us, the passion to be tied to a past which has meaning and significance and enables us to understand how we fit into the flow of mankind!

The genealogy bug has struck our family. A man named Leroy Fleagle in Anacoco, Louisiana, mailed to me the genealogical chart which traces our family tree back to Johann Valentin Fluegel who was born in 1716 in Germany. This type of chart holds both majesty and mystery. Some of the names represent people who were upstanding and other names represent people who couldn't always stand up so straight. Regardless, the names belong on the chart and give all the Fleagles on it a sense of community.

DECEMBER
2

The genealogy in Matthew's gospel communicates the flexibility of God's grace. The sovereign God has embraced the world, and within that embrace are some fascinating people, some famous and some infamous, but all connected to Jesus! Moffatt translated the beginning of Matthew 1:1 like this, "The birth roll of Jesus Christ."

As you examine this roll call, you will be impressed by the breadth and depth and width and height of God's immeasurable love! The scope of God's plan of salvation is powerfully illustrated by the birth roll of Jesus Christ. The rich and the poor, the young and the old, male and female, Jew and Gentile, all of these personalities are woven into His pedigree.

The celebration of Christmas is all-encompassing and all-inclusive. No one needs to stand outside the influence of the boy born in Bethlehem who grew up to be the Christ of the cross and the resurrected Redeemer. "Whosoever will may come!" There are no restrictions, no exemptions! The genealogy of Jesus Christ continues to add names to its roll call! I am grateful that my name has been inscribed, and everyone who accepts this priceless offer can be added to the birth roll of Jesus Christ.

There's plenty of room in the family!

OF THE FATHER'S LOVE BEGOTTEN

This is He whom seers in old time
Chanted of with one accord,
Whom the voices of the prophets
Promised in their faithful word;
Now He shines, the long expected;
Let creation praise its Lord,
Evermore and evermore.

Aurelius C. Prudentius

DEAR FATHER, *I am honored to be a member of Your family, one which includes every people, tribe and nation. Open a door to my world that others in my circle of influence may be adopted as sons and daughters of heaven.*

SONGS·OF·ADVENT

And Mary said:
"My soul glorifies the Lord and my spirit rejoices in God my Savior."

LUKE 1:46-47

'T<small>WAS</small> the day after Christmas and all through the house
Not a creature was happy, not even a mouse.
The daddy was grumbling; he looked in his poke;
His money was gone; he knew he was broke.
And Mommy was angry; the fridge was so full
Of leftover turkey, they'd eat until school
Had started again for the kids, whose tradition
Was to fume and to fuss, for the toys they'd petitioned
Were absent from under the tree Christmas day;
Oh, why do we celebrate the season this way!?!

DECEMBER 3

Christmas often turns into "Christmess." The stress and distress of too much money spent, too much food consumed, too much interaction with relatives, too little sleep, create a fatigue which does not reflect the joyful praise of the characters of the first Christmas. An examination of this most popular story finds its cast singing praise songs.

The "four songs of Christmas" are encountered in the world's most popular story. A teenage girl named Mary sang "The Magnificat;" an old man named Simeon supplied us with the "Nunc Dimittis," his swan song, for he praised God that he had seen the Deliverer even though it meant his imminent death. A priest named Zechariah could not accept the fact that his aged wife would become a new mother, and after John the Baptist's birth, he sang "The Benedictus." Finally we hear the angelic choir chanting "Gloria in Excelsis Deo," on the Judean hillsides, heralding a newborn child that was the visible picture of an invisible God. The first Christmas songs seasoned the birth of Christ with the spice of Christian joy. If you and I can sing the rapturous songs of redemption which have been written into the scores of our lives, we can make a difference in this Advent season.

A teenage girl, an aged priest and an ancient prayer warrior, plus an angelic ensemble—it was a coalition of praise. They all added to the glory of God that first Christmas! If I could give a gift to God's people it would be lips pulsating with praise—in our small towns, on our hillsides of work, as we worship in our churches and as we look upon on those who will hear our faith for the first time! Pray that you will drop notes of praise on someone's life this Christmas!

The question is not, "Can you sing?" The question is, "Do you have a song?"

IT CAME UPON THE MIDNIGHT CLEAR

It came upon the midnight clear,
That glorious song of old,
From angels bending near the earth,
To touch their harps of gold:
"Peace on the earth, good will to men,
From heaven's all gracious King."
The world in solemn stillness lay
To hear the angels sing.

Edmund H. Sears

DEAR FATHER, *make my life a symphony of praise. In the stormy panic of this holiday season, sing Your song to calm my heart.*

For nothing is impossible with God.

LUKE 1:37

CAN you believe in the impossible? The Christian faith invites you to go beyond the five senses, to let go of empirical thinking as an absolute indicator of reality and believe that the impossible can happen. Almighty God can intervene in life's traffic patterns, short-circuit natural law and superimpose the "Midas touch" on the fool's gold of this world, converting it into priceless treasure.

The Christmas story is a classic case of the impossible becoming possible. It cannot be logically explained. It is not rational. It is in the truest sense a mystery. A teenage virgin has a baby. A poor carpenter fills in as the father of the Creator. The impoverished couple cannot secure a room for the Messiah and end up in a cave in Bethlehem. Hillside shepherds are at the top of the guest list to see the newborn King. Gentile wise men get sidetracked on their journey to see Jesus and consult His enemies for advice on where to find Him.

The Heavenly Father's portfolio is pregnant with impossibilities!

He makes Adam out of dust particles. He conquers Egypt, perhaps the world's mightiest empire, through Moses' rod. He slays Goliath of Gath through the bravery of a young shepherd named David who is holding a

DECEMBER

4

slingshot and five stones from the river. The impossible flavors the three-and-one-half-year ministry of Jesus. Bland water is turned into the finest of wines. A little lad's lunch feeds a multitude of thousands. A mud pack heals the eyes of a blind man. A cross, a wretched and cruel Roman cross, becomes the saving symbol of Christendom.

Because nothing is too arduous, too difficult, too impossible for God, you and I can pick up our deflated dreams and carry them to Him. Look beyond the obvious ("It can't be done") to the actual reality ("He can do anything but fail").

Christmas was impossible, but God made it history!

It is a still night in Bethlehem and the silence is pierced with the cry of a newborn child. A humble manger holds a holy King! Angels are singing, Jewish shepherds are running, and a couple who have never consummated their marriage are smiling. A tiny baby has been born—a boy who will one day rock the religious establishment and perform unprecedented miracles. His death will open the door for anyone who believes in Him to live forever. Impossible? Not really; the Christmas diary confirms this resounding assurance, "But with God all things are possible!" (Matthew 19:26).

There is no such thing as "can't" with God.

ANGELS WE HAVE HEARD ON HIGH

Angels we have heard on high,
Sweetly singing o'er the plains,
And the mountains in reply
Echo back their joyous strains.
Gloria in Excelsis Deo,
Gloria in Excelsis Deo.

See within a manger laid
Jesus, Lord of heaven and earth!
Mary, Joseph, lend your aid,
With us sing our Saviour's birth.
Gloria in Excelsis Deo,
Gloria in Excelsis Deo.

French carol

DEAR HEAVENLY FATHER, *as I look closer at the Christmas story I am stunned by its improbabilities. Don't let me live by only sensory perception, but equip me to try and grasp goals which seem impossible.*

The Wardrobe of the Season

Blessed are
the pure in heart,
for they will see God.

MATTHEW 5:8

*I*T occurred one Thanksgiving season in our second grade Sunday school class. Our students were asked to fill out the feathers of their Thanksgiving turkey with praises and statements of gratitude to God. One boy piped up, "I'm thankful that I am a righteous dude!" Well, the vernacular is certainly contemporary, but the principle is ancient. God's people, inhabited by His Spirit, having access to the resources of redemptive faith, are to be pure people.

There is the distinct essence of purity in the lives of the characters of the first Christmas. God chose them to be vessels, through which His plan could flow powerfully and unimpeded. Sin, misplaced priorities, guilt and bitterness can clog the vessels of God causing constriction which forbids the free flow of God's love, mercy and faith.

A very special lady mothered the incarnate God. Though she was young, perhaps fourteen to sixteen years of age, though she was from a poverty-stricken, unimpressive town called Nazareth, Mary was God's preference.

Young lady, the Lord God Almighty is still recruiting young women who make Christianity the number one priority in their lives. The world desperately needs young women who are attractive internally as well as exter-

DECEMBER

5

nally. God wants ladies in the making, whose mouths are filled with praise, not profanity, and whose bodies are pure, not overused, worn-out dish rags.

We meet a married couple in this incredible Christmas drama who were involved in Jewish ministry, whose lives projected righteousness, but whose prayers had not been answered. The fullness of time came for Zechariah and Elizabeth. With the touch of God's miraculous Spirit, two achievements were reached in one swift stroke. This couple had a son, John the Baptist, and through him God's purpose for a messenger to prepare a way for the Savior was fulfilled.

My wardrobe is not just clothing!

Today we might use the word "upstanding" to describe Elizabeth and Zechariah, but in the Bible they are characterized as upright. They were strong to obey God's Word in its entirety. Their agenda was clear, and they were committed to it. The years did not dim their allegiance to their God. May it be said of our middle-age-and-up crowd, that the fires still burn and that the zeal has not taken a sabbatical. This husband and wife merit a description that I would cherish. Their vessels were uncluttered, and God poured His will into them and it was good.

Many of us want to be righteous dudes! Confess and commit yourself to God. He will surprise you with what He can pour through an uncluttered vessel.

O LITTLE TOWN OF BETHLEHEM

How silently, how silently
The wondrous Gift is given!
So God imparts to human hearts
The blessings of His heaven.
No ear may hear His coming,
But in this world of sin,
Where meek souls will receive Him, still
The dear Christ enters in.

Phillips Brooks

LORD,
You are the
ultimate tailor,
the premier
fashion designer.
Please consider me
as a model for You
during these days
leading up to
Christmas, which
will present
so many
opportunities for
social interaction.

His mercy extends to those who fear him, from generation to generation.

LUKE 1:50

*T*UCKED within the Christmas story is the unusual repetition of a key word which communicates God's response to sinful men. This word demands investigation. Sherlock Holmes needs to dust off his magnifying glass, Jim Rockford needs to turn the key in his Camaro and you and I need to start digging for treasure. In Luke 1, a section which covers only twenty-nine verses, the word mercy appears several times. This is unparalleled in the New Testament. Could it be that the inspired writer was trying to ensure that his readers would grasp the essence of the incarnation, God's trip to earth down the staircase of heaven with a baby folded in His arms? I believe there is a trail for the church to follow, a message that the sovereign God did not want us to leave undiscovered. This Christmas story is decorated with the mercy of God and this Christmas season should be adorned with the manifestation of mercy by His children.

DECEMBER

6

Mercy is active compassion. It is not a sterile sympathy, but a "Good Samaritan" sympathy that does not walk by as did the priest and the Levite in the biblical account of the beaten traveler on his way from Jerusalem to Jericho. A.W. Tozer defined mercy as "an attribute of God, an infinite and inexhaustible energy within the divine nature which disposes God to be actively compassionate (*The Knowledge of the Holy*, p. 90). God's hand doesn't just wave, it disperses food to the hungry, comfort to the bereaved, forgiveness to the transgressor. God's mercy is active, not dormant compassion.

Don't miss this attribute of God. Don't miss this loud and noisy message of Christmas: God is merciful and has demonstrated this attribute through the issuing of His Son to us. He is actively compassionate which is vividly demonstrated through Jesus Christ. This Jesus "came to pay a debt He did not owe because we owed a debt we could not pay" (from a Christmas card).

Give God's gift of mercy to those in need this Christmas.

This Christmas season you will encounter individuals who need help from someone who not only acknowledges their need but reacts and responds to satisfy it! You will have to break your routine long enough to address the wounds of a hurting person; you will have to pick up the phone and share a word of prayer; you will have to buy a small gift and alter your itinerary to visit a sick friend; you will have to have enough mercy to share the good news that forgiveness is available and accessible through Jesus Christ.

Christmas provides a prime-time opportunity for the disbursement of mercy! Billy Graham challenges us with these relevant words: "When confronted with the world's problems, we Christians say automatically, `Christianity is the answer.' But this is not true. It is the application of Christianity which is the answer."

THERE'S A WIDENESS IN GOD'S MERCY

There's a wideness in God's mercy,
Like the wideness of the sea;
There's a kindness in His justice,
Which is more than liberty.

Frederick W. Faber

DEAR LORD OF ALL MANKIND, *forgive me for not disbursing Your mercy. Lead me to a person this season who desperately needs my personal touch of care and compassion. Teach me the gospel of giving when so many are immersed in the gospel of getting.*

MESSIAH
in a
manger

And she gave birth to her firstborn, a son.
She wrapped him in cloths and placed him in a manger,
because there was no room for them in the inn.

LUKE 2:7

*I*N *The Chronicles of Narnia,* C.S. Lewis wrote this summary of Christmas spoken through one of his characters: "A stable once held something inside that was bigger than our whole world." As the shepherds gazed into that feeding trough called a manger their eyes focused on a Messiah, a Deliverer, the King of kings.

The drawing board of heaven had fashioned a most incredible scenario. God would descend into humanity and wrap Himself in human flesh. The Eternal One would subject Himself to the limitations of time and space with the journey beginning in a virgin's vacant and untried womb.

Why would God wrap His Son in baby clothes? Bishop Fulton Sheen proposed this opinion:

Man cannot love anything he cannot get his arms around, and the universe is too immense. That is why the Almighty had to become a babe whom we could encircle in our arms and thus make religion lovable.

Christmas is the celebration of God's descent into humanity. The theological term is incarnation, "God becoming flesh." And though on the night of His birth Jesus may have seemed vulnerable, His mission would

DECEMBER
7

demonstrate a strength and a power the world had never witnessed before. Mary Alderidge's poem projects a warning:

> *I saw a stable low and bare*
> *A little child in a manger . . .*
> *The safety of the world was lying there*
> *And the world's danger.*

This Holy One of God had humble beginnings but before He was through on earth, the powers of darkness would tremble. Demons would run from Him, stormy seas would coo like a baby and death's door would be yanked open, allowing those who were confined by it to live again.

At Christmas the beauty of the baby is to be admired, but to stop at the manger is to miss the message. This baby grew up. The kitten became the Lion of the Tribe of Judah. Look carefully, reflectively, reverently at this baby named Jesus. Don't be mesmerized by His innocence or be sympathetic toward the inauspiciousness of His first night of life. As you see that baby, look beyond His first day on earth to a temple cleansing, the feeding of thousands with a small boy's lunch and His resurrection from the land of the dead. This baby was born into a manger so that one day, by the Holy Spirit, He could be born again in your heart. Doug Benner tendered this powerful analogy:

The manger of Bethlehem cradled a Messiah!

And just as You were born into a crude and inhospitable world, You allow
Your Holy Spirit to be born into our human hearts—hearts which often are not
any warmer or more welcoming to You than that stable was to Mary and
Joseph—hearts which contain our own personal beasts.

Who was born that first Christmas night? The answer resonates through the tunnels of time, "A Savior who is Christ the Lord!"

THERE'S A SONG IN THE AIR

There's a tumult of joy
O'er the wonderful birth,
For a Virgin's sweet Boy
Is the Lord of the earth.
Ay! the star rains its fire
while the beautiful sing,
For the manger of Bethlehem
cradles a King!

Josiah G. Holland

DEAR LORD JESUS, *Your love has been demonstrated in your descent to Bethlehem's manger. I acknowledge that You were born not only in a manger but You have been born again in my heart. I pray that as the shepherds saw You in the manger others may see You in me.*

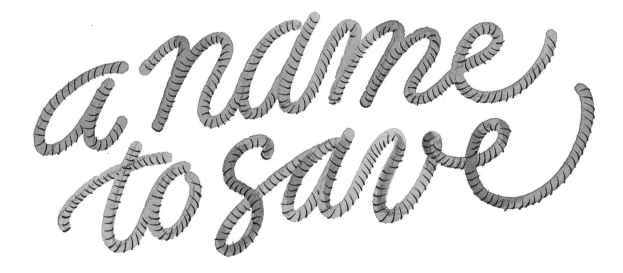

She will give birth to a son,
and you are to give him the name Jesus,
because he will save his people from their sins.

MATTHEW 1:21

*O*NE of the most significant and agonizing decisions that a couple makes is the selection of a name for their child. The naming of a child in biblical times often communicated a child's purpose or described a character trait or preserved a memory from birth. For example, when Rachel gave birth to Esau and Jacob, the second boy emerged holding on to his older brother's heel. They named him Jacob meaning, "he grasps the heel."

Andrew Murray provides insight on this subject of name selection:

> *What's in a person's name? It is a word of expression in which a person is represented to us. When I mention or hear a name it brings to mind the whole man, what I know of him, and also the impression he has made on me.*

What name would be attached to the Son of God, the firstborn of all creation, the visible picture of the invisible God? The name chosen should embrace His mission, His ministry, His destiny. Mary and Joseph were not given the privilege or obligation to choose the baby's name, for "On the eighth day, when it was time to circumcise him, he was named Jesus, the name the angel had given him before he had been conceived" (Luke 2:21).

The Word of God records over 100 names for the Son of the Most High God, but the name Jesus has become the primary way we address the Savior of the world. Jesus means "the Lord saves," and indeed it embraces His purpose for coming to Bethlehem's manger, for being suspended from Calvary's cross and for emerging from Joseph of Arimathea's tomb.

Each time the name of Jesus is spoken God's love is conveyed for a fallen world. It spreads and sprinkles over our existence the message of hope, the promise of a better future.

God named His Son Jesus— "the Lord saves!"

This is a name which shuttles to our lives salvation and suffering, healing and harm. It is a name in which we pray and the name that is applied at our baptism. It is the most honored name in the universe—Jesus. Jesus Christ Himself, along with Peter, Paul and other New Testament writers made extensive efforts to convince us of the promises and pain we would encounter because we believed, promoted and identified with the name, Jesus.

How exalted is this name? In Paul's letter to the saints at Philippi he wrote: "Therefore God exalted him to the highest place and gave him the name that is above every name, that at the name of Jesus every knee should bow, in heaven and on earth and under the earth" (2:9-10).

What did you say was that baby's name? His name is Jesus!

SEEKING FOR ME!

Jesus, my Saviour, to Bethlehem came,
Born in a manger to sorrow and shame;
Oh, it was wonderful—blest be His name!
Seeking for me, for me!
Seeking for me, for me!
Seeking for me, for me!
Oh, it was wonderful—blest be His name!
Seeking for me, for me!

Anonymous

DEAR JESUS, *my lips have so often spoken Your name. I am so glad that its meaning has touched my life. I honor you as Savior, Sanctifier, Healer and Coming King.*

the five little fingers of God

So the other disciples told [Thomas], "We have seen the Lord!"
But he said to them, "Unless I see the nail marks in his hands
and put my finger where the nails were, and put my hand into his side,
I will not believe it."

JOHN 20:25

*I*T is natural for the mother of a newborn to take the baby's hand and count its fingers. Mary of Nazareth must have extended a broad smile as she clutched that soft, tiny hand and found that she counted five fingers.

As we worship this Christmas season, we must be reminded that the hands of that holy infant had a manifest destiny. They would be critical instruments in God's plan to visit and transform His creation. Through those hands would flow an explosive power which has never been duplicated. They were holy hands, heavenly hands and on that special night a teenage maiden held something very special. For when she grasped that little hand, she grasped the five little fingers of God.

DECEMBER
9

The hands of Jesus grew to be the tools of a carpenter's son. However, beyond that distinction they served as agents of a miraculous Messiah. Jesus performed radical healings with those hands, such as when He touched the unclean lepers. Those hands ushered light to the blind and strength to crippled legs. To the widow of Nain, those hands brought resurrection life to her dead boy. Jesus' hands touched the terrified disciples on the Mountain of Transfiguration as He invited them to "Get up. . . . Don't be afraid" (Matthew 17:7). When little children were brought to Him He touched them and blessed them.

Those hands were also abused by His enemies. Those hands, at one time small and smooth, were one day large and red as they carried the cross and then were nailed to it. And proof of Jesus' resurrection from the dead was validated by those who viewed the nail prints in His hands. His invitation to Thomas to look at the evidence included those hands, "Put your finger here; see my hands. Reach out your hand and put it into my side. Stop doubting and believe" (John 20:27). When Jesus ascended to heaven those hands were employed for one final blessing:

Jesus' hands were the fingers of God!

> When he had led them out to the vicinity of Bethany, he lifted up his hands and blessed them. While he was blessing them, he left them and was taken up into heaven. Then they worshiped him and returned to Jerusalem with great joy. (Luke 24:50-52)

And in Revelation, the Bible's climactic book, Jesus' hands are deemed the only hands worthy of opening the book sealed with seven seals.

Don't just admire the marshmallow texture of the hands of the baby of Bethlehem. Watch those hands march into the context of ministry, be nailed to a rugged, splintered cross and eventually cherish the crown of heaven. The five fingers of God touched earth and man, and neither have ever been the same.

YESTERDAY, TODAY, FOREVER

Oft on earth He healed the sufferer
By His mighty hand;
Still our sicknesses and sorrows
Go at His command.
He who gave His healing virtue
To a woman's touch,
To the faith that claims His fullness
Still will give as much.
Yesterday, today, forever, Jesus is the same;
All may change, but Jesus never! Glory to His name!
Glory to His name; Glory to His name;
All may change, but Jesus never! Glory to His name.

Albert B. Simpson

DEAR FATHER, *Jesus Christ has touched me. He has healed my soul. He has given me new life. Lead my feet to those that I can touch with compassionate hands. May my hands be instruments to show love to those in pain this current Christmas season.*

GIFTS
LEFT
UNDER
THE TREE

For everyone who has will be given more, and he will have an abundance.
Whoever does not have, even what he has will be taken from him.

MATTHEW 25:29

PERISH the thought of leaving gifts under the tree. It's unthinkable! Someone spent a lot of time shopping for those gifts, and expended money to buy them, and specifically put special wrapping paper around them to enhance their attractiveness! Yet, gifts will be left under a lot of trees this year. No, I'm not referring to Christmas trees, for I'm certain that all of those gifts will be happily unwrapped and cheerfully received. I'm referring to the trees of our lives for the Bible often refers to our lives that way. Take a look under your tree; there may still be some unwrapped gifts waiting for you to open and cheerfully receive!

Matthew 25:29 does not seem quite fair; the one who has more will be given even more, while the one not having much will be stripped of what he has and that will be distributed to the one having much. It appears to promote the idea that the rich get richer and the poor get poorer.

As we examine the Word of God and even our own lives, there are times when this philosophy is justified! If you choose to be poor and not take advantage of your opportunities, then you deserve to be destitute. Let me illustrate. In our family there were times at the table when for some reason one of us boys refused to eat his piece of steak. Mother, sensing that the

DECEMBER
10

steak would be wasted, passed it on to another son. One refused to eat the meat and enjoy it, so by choice he remained unnourished! Another who had cheerfully eaten the T-bone, would be given an extra portion. So in God's kingdom, the gifts are under the tree. It is you and I who choose whether we will enjoy them or reject them and have them passed to someone else.

The word "gift" is prevalent in the Bible. The words "gift" and "gifts" each appear over eighty times. The verb appears in even greater frequency. So we may draw the appropriate conclusion that God is greatly interested in gifts.

God, the most worthy, has given His very best gift, Jesus Christ, to a fallen world. Many people won't open the gift because they don't feel worthy. However a gift does not depend on the worth of the receiver but on the love of the giver. Don't wait to be worthy, just accept the gracious gift of the Heavenly Father—the best gift of all, Jesus.

Jesus is the ultimate Christmas gift!

HARK, THE HERALD ANGELS SING

Hail, the heaven-born Price of Peace!
Hail, the Sun of Righteousness!
Light and life to all He brings,
Risen with healing in His wings.
Mild He lays His glory by,
Born that man no more may die,
Born to raise the sons of earth,
Born to give them second birth.
Hark, the herald angels sing,
"Glory to the newborn King."

Charles Wesley

DEAR FATHER, *I aspire to be a distributor of the greatest gift that could be given. Position me so that I can help those who need to open it have that opportunity.*

Glory to God in the highest,
and on earth peace to men on whom his favor rests.

LUKE 2:14

*H*ENRY WADSWORTH LONGFELLOW wrote the words to the famous Christmas carol "I Heard the Bells on Christmas Day." Listen to the third stanza which painfully declares the great poet's sorrow:

And in despair I bowed my head:
"There is no peace on earth," I said,
"For hate is strong and mocks the song
Of peace on earth, good will to men."

Over twenty-seven centuries ago a prophet named Isaiah predicted the birth of a child. He complimented the child with a roll call of names. In Isaiah 9:6 we read:

DECEMBER
11

For to us a child is born, to us a son is given, and the government will be on his shoulders. And he will be called Wonderful Counselor, Mighty God, Everlasting Father, Prince of Peace.

It is this final title, *Prince of Peace,* which addresses Longfellow's despair.

In the well-known Christmas story, a choir of angels sang this marvelous refrain, very appropriate and very much in line with Isaiah's prediction of the Deliverer's role: "Glory to God in the highest, and on earth peace to men on whom his favor rests."

In very real terms, Jesus Christ was the peace child. I once saw a bumper sticker which supports this very assertion. It read like this:

Know Jesus, Know Peace.
No Jesus, No Peace.

It was Augustine who said, "My heart is restless until it rests in Thee." Pascal wrote: "There is a hole in every man's soul and only God can fill it." I would propose that there is a manger in every man's heart, and Jesus Christ desires to occupy it!

Don and Carol Richardson ventured into the rain forest in order to convey the good news of Jesus Christ to primitive people. They discovered that the account of Judas betraying Jesus delighted them because they applauded treachery and rewarded it. Polluted hearts eventually led the tribe to be divided against itself and a civil war ensued. The battles persisted until one chief took a drastic step; he offered his son as a sacrifice for peace. His son became the peace child. In Christmas, God also has presented us with a Peace Child!

Jesus
is
the
Peace
Child!

I HEARD THE BELLS ON CHRISTMAS DAY

Then pealed the bells more loud and deep:
"God is not dead, nor doth he sleep;
The wrong shall fail, the right prevail,
With peace on earth, good will to men."

Till, ringing, singing on its way,
The world revolved from night to day,
A voice, a chime, a chant sublime,
Of peace on earth, good will to men.

Henry W. Longfellow

DEAR PEACEMAKER, *I need to lay down my arms before You. Bring a truce in my life when I am warring against Your word, Your will, Your way. And though the culture that embraces me is in great turmoil, may I manifest Your perfect peace in the midst of earthly chaos.*

And there were shepherds living out in the fields nearby,
keeping watch over their flocks at night. An angel of the Lord appeared to them,
and the glory of the Lord shone around them, and they were terrified.

LUKE 2:8-9

*I*WORKED the night shift, or the "graveyard shift" as it is sometimes called, when I was earning my way through college. It was the shift that I appreciated the least. The night hours dragged on and on like waiting room stints in a doctor's office. When I left work in the morning and ventured out into the daylight, other humans were walking briskly to their places of employment while I was looking for a place to collapse and take a long nap. Night shift made me feel as if most of the world was going west and I was headed dead east.

The Christmas story includes a group of shepherds working the night shift. It was another night and another denarius. One more vigil in a seemingly incessant streak of after-sunset assignments. But this night shift would be dramatically different. This night shift would change them and rearrange them. This night shift would explode with front page news and a sprint to Bethlehem to see the Savior of the world.

You may think your day shifts are just like night shifts. The alarm goes off at its appointed time and its harsh personality never changes. You drive the same route to your place of employment. You interact with the same demographic grid of coworkers. Your lunch is easily memorized and

DECEMBER
12

becomes a boring nutritional necessity. One more day to add to the perpetual pilgrimage into the ordinary which you must travel with little variation. But, think about this: If you had a "divine moment" when the reality of the supernatural intersected with your natural life, wouldn't that change the complexion of your daily experience?

It certainly made the mundane take on majesty for those first-century shepherds. Their fear climbed like mercury over a Bunsen burner. Their joy escalated like a jet during takeoff. They were running and rejoicing, traveling and telling, worshiping and wondering. The birth of Jesus Christ changed their lives forever. From that moment on, their night shifts would tingle with memories of their encounter with God's Son. Their expectations of what might happen and the reality of what did happen left them dreaming of what could happen.

Christmas changed the complexion of history for all who participated in this incredible moment. The coming of Christ to a human heart has that same transforming power. If you desire a life full of adventure, if you long for the pursuit of excellence and if you want to make a difference in your world, then open your heart to Jesus. Revelation 3:20 issues an invitation: "Here I am! I stand at the door and knock. If anyone hears my voice and opens the door, I will come in and eat with him, and he with me." If your heart is Christ's home the darkness will turn to light, and the night shift

Let the birth of Jesus change your life forever.

atmosphere will take on a whole new significance. "The shepherds returned, glorifying and praising God for all the things they had heard and seen, which were just as they had been told" (Luke 2:20). It all started on a night shift. Oh, what a night!

WHILE SHEPHERDS WATCHED THEIR FLOCKS BY NIGHT

While shepherds watched their flocks by night,
All seated on the ground,
The angel of the Lord came down,
And glory shone around,
And glory shone around.

"Fear not," said he—for mighty dread
Had seized their troubled mind—
"Glad tidings of great joy I bring
To you and all mankind,
To you and all mankind."

Nahum Tate

FATHER,
I want to be
animated like the
shepherds
on that first
Christmas night.
I ask that Your
majesty might
invade my life and
energize my body,
mind and soul.
This Christmas
season may my
hurry be connected
to the spreading
of the "good news"
concerning
Your Son.

The Pseudo-King

When King Herod heard this he was disturbed, and all Jerusalem with him.

MATTHEW 2:3

*T*HE birth of Jesus in Bethlehem was not a joyous occasion for Herod the Great. He was the Christmas story's "Grinch." Even more tragic is the reality of his jealousy and murderous treachery which emerged from his insecurity as king.

Herod the Great did not inherit his throne, rather he was appointed to it by the Roman Empire. He was a non-Jew who was ruling over the Jews of Judea. He had the title but not the respect of his subjects. His legacy is one of monumental building programs mixed with the habitual murdering of enemies and even his own family members. His architectural achievements included theaters, fortresses and this royal rogue was the catalyst for the rebuilding of the temple in Jerusalem, which began in 19 B.C. and was finished posthumously. But his hit list encompassed his wife, her mother, his three sons, his brother-in-law and his most infamous project remains the massacre of the male babies of Bethlehem.

DECEMBER
13

The Magi from the East had followed the special star which had been hung over Jesus' birthplace. They made their journey to King Herod and then, with what seems to be blatant audacity, asked him this question: "Where is the one who has been born king of the Jews?" (Matthew 2:2). In other words, they confronted the King with the question, "Where is the real king?" The Magi's inquiry was dangerously close to treason. They gained an audience with the King of the Jews and then requested that the pseudo-king direct them to the real King.

Herod moved to answer their question. He consulted with the chief priests and teachers of the law and they informed him that Bethlehem had been prophesied by the prophet Micah. He then lied to them about his motives, "Go and make a careful search for the child. As soon as you find him, report to me, so that I too may go and worship him" (Matthew 2:8). Herod did not desire to worship Jesus; he aimed to terminate this threat to the throne.

It seems that a monarch would not be threatened by a tiny child, but Herod's awareness of his illegitimacy as the King of Judea and the dark side of his personality led him to react with violence and inhumanity when the Magi didn't report back to him with the location of this future king.

The monster of Christmas ordered that all male babies in Bethlehem and its hinterlands who were two years old or younger were to be slain in an attempt to eradicate a potential competitor for the throne. Demographers estimate that this area had a population around 2,000, which meant that approximately twenty-five babies would comprise his death list. Women

Let's bow down and worship Jesus, the King.

wept bitterly, babies bled profusely but Herod failed to extinguish the flame of the new King.

Herod could have been a hero. Instead, he chose to be one of history's largest heels. He could have worshiped Jesus, but he chose to conspire against Him. Herod assumes Satan's attitude from Milton's *Paradise Lost*, "Better to reign in hell than serve in heaven" (l. 262). The Magi were highly regarded in their society but they chose to bow down and worship Jesus. Herod was also draped in prestige and affluence, but he selected a different road. He would not worship Jesus Christ and proceeded to discover that when you fight against God's plans, you lose royally. Each Christmas men and women choose their response to Jesus Christ. What will your choice be? Will you bow down and bless Him or will you stand up and curse Him?

JOY TO THE WORLD

He rules the earth with truth and grace,
And makes the nations prove
The glories of His righteousness,
And wonders of His love,
And wonders of His love,
And wonders, wonders of His love.

Isaac Watts

DEAR LORD JESUS, *I choose to worship You. My heart bows down before You. I lay down my life and all its resources before Your presence. You have brought me such joy; may my life bring You pleasure and blessing.*

hitching
your hopes to a star

After Jesus was born in Bethlehem in Judea, during the time of King Herod,
Magi from the east came to Jerusalem and asked,
"Where is the one who has been born king of the Jews?
We saw his star in the east and have come to worship him."

MATTHEW 2:1-2

*T*HE story of Christmas has been embellished in many ways, but no aspect of the world's most popular story has been added to more profoundly than the visit of the Magi.

The carol "We Three Kings of Orient Are" is a classic example of adding to or twisting a text. First, these men were not kings, they were Magi. Magi represented a high level priestly group in Medo-Persia. They had interests in medicine, religion, astronomy, astrology and divination. Second, they were not from the Orient or Far East. All evidence points to a Mesopotamian or Persian location in the area of modern Iran, a distance of 650 miles from Jerusalem and Bethlehem. Third, we are not certain of the number. Three men are presumed because of the three gifts, but the Bible never states the number. In fact, some early traditions set the number at twelve.

DECEMBER
14

God captured the attention of these stargazers with an extraordinary constellation, the star designated as the special and unique star of the King of the Jews. These Magi made the long and arduous journey led by this heavenly light. They knew that the King awaited them but they were uncertain as to His exact location. They approached King Herod for guidance, and although he did not know the answer, he summoned scholars who informed him that in the book of Micah, Bethlehem was predicted as the birthplace of this ruler.

The star provided further guidance and these Magi followed its light to the house where the young child was now in residence.

The very sight of this star sent their joy spiraling, but this did not equal the worship which emerged from their encounter with this child King.

What will you give Jesus in honor of His birth?

As they bowed down and worshiped Jesus, they presented three gifts both rare and expensive: gold, frankincense and myrrh. Gold was the world's most precious mineral commodity. Frankincense, a fragrant gum resin, was burned by the priesthood in temple worship. Myrrh, the orange-colored resin, utilized in cosmetics and perfumes, served as a pain-killer and embalming substance.

These Gentile travelers are remembered for their gifts, significant and expensive tokens of their worship. They didn't search for Jesus for what they could receive from Him; they diligently sought Him to deliver special tributes worthy of His person and mission.

What are you willing to give to Jesus Christ this Christmas season? Here are some items on Jesus' Christmas list:

1. *Quality time spent with parents, children and spouse.*
2. *The investment in a ministry which teaches men and women, boys and girls about the kingdom of God and its King.*
3. *A forgiving spirit directed toward one who has hurt you.*
4. *Lips which are quick to praise and slow to criticize.*
5. *A renewed commitment to daily interact with God through personal devotions.*
6. *Climbing through a window of opportunity when God creates one to witness to someone who does not know your Savior personally.*
7. *A prayer ministry wrapped in compassion and concern for others within and without your family structure.*

These gifts are not cheap, they demand time and talents and treasures, but their unwrapping will bring joy to the face of a king—King Jesus.

WHAT CHILD IS THIS, WHO LAID TO REST?

So bring Him incense, gold and myrrh,
Come, peasant, king, to own Him;
The King of kings salvation brings,
Let loving hearts enthrone Him.
Raise, raise the song on high,
The Virgin sings her lullaby:
Joy, joy, for Christ is born,
The Babe, the Son of Mary!

English carol

DEAR KING JESUS, *I come to worship You, to give and not receive. Show me the gifts that will please You most this Christmas season and enable me to give them joyfully.*

the color Red

*In him we have redemption through his blood, the forgiveness of sins,
in accordance with the riches of God's grace.*

EPHESIANS 1:7

*T*HE Christmas celebration decorates our cities, our churches and our homes with the color red. The poinsettias, candy canes, holly berries, candles, Christmas stockings, Santa's suit and Rudolph's nose all bear witness to the indisputable fact that red is the color of Christmas.

Red is fundamental in the biblical color scheme. The Old Testament uses this color to describe Esau's body at birth (Gen. 25:25), the stew which Jacob traded for Esau's birthright (Gen. 25:30), the covering of the Tabernacle which was composed of ram skins (Exodus 26:14), the face of Job which resulted from his prolific weeping (Job 16:16), the dangerous wine of wisdom literature (Proverbs 23:31) and the sins of the people (Isaiah 1:18). The New Testament features Jesus' analogy of a red sky to illustrate how the signs of the times are interpreted (Matthew 16:2) and the fiery red horse of Revelation carries a rider who prompts men to slay each other (6:4).

DECEMBER
15

The color red has been prominent in Christendom primarily because it has symbolized the redeeming blood of Jesus Christ which cleanses the hearts of believing sinners. It should not be overlooked that the Christmas story is sprinkled with references to redemption obtained through the incarnation of Jesus Christ. Red is very appropriate for this season because of this undeniable connection. His birth embraced the concept of His death, for He was born to die!

Just prior to Jesus' birth, Zechariah, John the Baptist's father and a priest, spoke of God's Son in these terms, "Praise be to the Lord, the God of Israel, because he has come and has redeemed his people" (Luke 1:68). Eight days after His birth, Jesus' parents brought Him to be circumcised and His blood was shed to tattoo this male child with the sign of the covenant (Luke 2:21). At His dedication, the aged Simeon spoke to Mary of future bloodletting in her soul, "And a sword will pierce your own soul too" (Luke 2:35). Immediately after Simeon's prediction, Anna enters the temple area and Luke writes, "Coming up to them at that very moment, she gave thanks to God and spoke about the child to all who were looking forward to the redemption of Jerusalem" (Luke 2:38). Herod's attempt to eradicate the King of the Jews by destroying all male babies under the age of two meant that red blood would flow from the tiniest citizens of David's prophetic city.

Jesus was born to die, to pay the price for our sins.

We worship Christ at Christmas because His advent liberates us from the bondage of our sins. The redness of His blood releases us from our erratic past and redirects us into an eternal future with immeasurable hope! That is why the Heavenly Father wove red throughout the fabric of Christmas.

LET ALL MORTAL FLESH KEEP SILENCE

Let all mortal flesh keep silence,
And with fear and trembling stand;
Ponder nothing earthly-minded,
For with blessing in His hand,
Christ our God to earth descendeth,
Our full homage to demand.

King of kings, yet born of woman,
As of old on earth He stood,
Lord of lords, in human vesture—
In the body and the blood—
He will give to all the faithful
His own self for heavenly food.

Liturgy of St. James (sixth century)

DEAR
AUTHOR
OF THE
CHRISTMAS
STORY,
I worship You
for the act of
redemption. You
placed the
purchase price in a
humble manger.
You provided for
me the shedding of
blood which was
imperative for a
new beginning, a
new birth.

A White Christmas

"Come now, let us reason together," says the LORD.
"Though your sins are like scarlet, they shall be as white as snow;
though they are red as crimson, they shall be like wool."

ISAIAH 1:18

*T*HERE are many people who are wishing for a white Christmas this year. Irving Berlin's song, "White Christmas," has planted in all of us a sentimental seed that those shimmering ice crystals will find frozen air and reach the winter ground giving our holiday a white blanket.

Did you know it only snows on one-third of the earth's surface? People who live in the polar regions witness snow in all the seasons. Those who reside in the temperate zone watch for it only in winter. Those who make their home in the tropics may have never seen it. We may safely conclude that most of earth's inhabitants will not have a white Christmas!

Was the first Christmas white? Though some of our Christmas cards depict the brave couple from Nazareth courageously making their way to Bethlehem through a harsh and wintry blizzard, the actual chances that Jesus Christ was born into a winter wonderland are slim. We dare not say impossible, for it does snow in the Jerusalem area about three or four days each winter. Some winters are exceptionally white. In January of 1950, twenty inches of snow fell in the area where Jesus was born. In February of 1920, twenty-nine inches fell from the skies over the place where Jesus lay. However, these are rare occurrences and make the thought of a white

DECEMBER
16

first Christmas a remote possibility!

There is an excellent chance that "all your Christmases be white" if you look at Christmas through the eyeglass of Scripture. The analogy of snow is fairly frequent in Scripture and may guarantee that anyone may experience a white Christmas.

Physical snow does appear in Scripture. In Second Samuel 23:20 it is recorded that Benaiah slew a lion in a pit in the time of snow. The Lord God Almighty inserted snow into Scripture to speak of glistening white. In Daniel's vision of the "Ancient of Days," his garments were snow-white and his hair the same. We find a recurrence of this description in Revelation 1:14 in reference to Jesus Christ.

Let heaven's snow wash away your scarlet stains.

Scripture also uses snow as a word picture for spiritual cleansing. It is in this context that everyone may have a white Christmas on their annual agenda.

David kept his many sins unconfessed surrounding the death of Uriah, Bathsheba's husband, and his subsequent adultery with this beautiful woman. When Nathan, the prophet, confronted him with his sin, David was shattered; his pride collapsed and his spiritual side took over. He then wrote the words of Psalm 51:7, "Wash me, and I will be whiter than snow."

Isaiah, the monumental prophet of the Old Testament, spoke these words from the Lord to a disobedient and deluded people in Judah,

"Come now, let us reason together," says the LORD. "Though your sins are like scarlet, they shall be as white as snow; though they are red as crimson, they shall be like wool." (Isaiah 1:18)

Scarlet is the most difficult stain to remove from garments. It is obstinate, and often if it finds its way into a piece of clothing, that item will be marked forever. Spiritual scarlet poses a more indelible mark. In spite of what we can't do, God offers a solution. Let Him who made the garment do the dry cleaning! Let Him cleanse the heart that He made for Himself. Let Him salvage what we are ready to throw away. Give Him your scarlet stains and He will give you a blanket of blessing, a white blanket of snow which will cover your heart.

Do you want a white Christmas? It is as sure as the promises of God. Let that wonderful love of God fall softly on the dry and thirsty ground of your soul and you will possess a purity that is whiter than the freshest snow that has ever kissed the earth.

WHITER THAN SNOW

Lord Jesus, I long to be perfectly whole;
I want Thee forever to live in my soul.
Break down every idol, cast out every foe;
Now wash me, and I shall be whiter than snow.

James L. Nicholson

DEAREST FATHER,

I aspire to please You, to stand before You this Christmas with a clean and holy heart. Please allow the snow of heaven to fall softly on my heart so that I may have a white Christmas and so that others may enjoy the beauty of Your Holy Spirit made manifest in me.

UNDERSTANDING The Gift

For God so loved the world that he gave his one and only Son,
that whoever believes in him shall not perish but have eternal life.
For God did not send his Son into the world to condemn the world,
but to save the world through him.

JOHN 3:16-17

*I*N 1993 when we were home for Thanksgiving in Virginia, I looked through some of my brother-in-law's magazines and one was titled, *Modern Maturity*. Inside the front cover was a huge advertisement with a headline that hit me very hard, "Sometimes you don't get what you pay for. You get more." They were making a pitch for the New Yorker Salon, but my thoughts raced to the idea of grace, God's gift which cannot be earned by me or anyone else. And because of this season we call Christmas, we receive much more than we paid for.

The gift of Jesus Christ, born of a teenage virgin and adopted by a carpenter named Joseph, is grace personified at its best. Paul described this gift as "indescribable" in Second Corinthians 9:15. This is a season where giving is the theme and gifts are the focus. In this Christmas season I want us to take time to understand the gift! And one step further, I want us to open the gift. For if the gift is not received, it has no value for us.

It is very difficult for our modern culture to comprehend the gifts God gives to humanity. We sometimes give gifts at Christmas because other people give gifts to us. Some of us even calculate how much someone else gave, and then we return to them a gift comparable to what was given to

DECEMBER

17

us. (This is kind of a positive *lex talionis*, a happy "eye for an eye.")

The biblical words for gift portray a very different attitude. The two key words in the New Testament present the idea of unmerited, unearned, undeserved gifts. The first word *doron* (verb), or its noun cousin *dorea*, stresses the "free gift," a gift gratuitous in character. The second word is *charisma*, a word that transferred straight into our English language. We speak of those who have charisma as those who are gifted in some special way. The original word, according to *Vine's Expository Dictionary of New Testament Words*, is "a gift of grace, a gift involving grace on the part of God as donor."

Our heavenly Father is not Ebenezer Scrooge. He is not stingy in gift-giving. When certain family members draw our names for the family Christmas gift exchange, we smile with delight, but when others draw our names, our smiles turn to frowns. God makes the former list, not the latter.

A gift is intended to be unwrapped and enjoyed!

And, His Son, quoted in Acts 20:35, left us this clue as to the nature of God: "It is more blessed to give than to receive." God is a splendid giver, a joyful giver, the world's number one giver. At Christmas we loudly sing and preach and read of His incredible object lesson laid in Bethlehem's manger. God became flesh and dwelt among us!

God gave at Christmas His very best, His own Son. He was sent into the despair of this earth resolved to brighten the darkness of our hearts. That baby's cry in Bethlehem signaled the arrival of a package so powerful, so unspeakable, so miraculous, that this gift, in the person of Jesus, could be unwrapped and the world would forever change.

The best gift of all is Jesus. He waits for you to open His gift of love, joy, peace and pardon for the first time! He came in order to reconcile God to man and man to man. A gift unopened is a tragedy. A gift refused is a pitiful circumstance. Open the gift, or as believers reopen the gift!

My brother-in-law was recently required to have a kidney transplant. What would you say if I told you a donor was found who was willing to risk his life in donating a kidney, but my brother-in-law George refused to accept the gift of this precious organ? What a tragedy! God has offered to be the donor and His Son is the gift! Do you understand that God offers more than you could ever pay for, more than you could ever dream of? Let's open the gift, the best gift of all, Jesus!

ONCE IN ROYAL DAVID'S CITY

He came down to earth from heaven
Who is God and Lord of all,
And His shelter was a stable,
And His cradle was a stall;
With the poor, and mean, and lowly,
Lived on earth our Saviour holy.

Cecil F.H. Alexander

DEAR LOVING FATHER, help me never to leave any of Your gifts unwrapped. I want to maximize all that You place into my life, each opportunity, each resource, each blessing. Show me any gift that I need to open this Christmas season.

a son away from home

The Word became flesh and made his dwelling among us.
We have seen his glory, the glory of the One and Only,
who came from the Father, full of grace and truth.

JOHN 1:14

WILL you be home for Christmas this year? Those who step over the threshold of their old home discover hugs, kisses and tears of joy which had been stored away for such an occasion! Christmas at home barrages the soul with a flood of memories: stories, some as worn as an old shoe sole, some as fresh as the ink on today's paper; a tree to decorate, with a collection of old and new ornaments; festive food, football games and falling snow; the candlelight service. The joys of the past, present and future seem simultaneously focused in a Christmas at home.

There are some who can't sing "I'll Be Home for Christmas" this year. A lonely serviceman stationed on a strange shore will reread a perfumed letter over and over dreaming of the love and warmth of Christmas at home. A college student high on hopes but down on dollars is forced to wait on tables while Christmas turkey is served back home. An expectant mother, expanded in body, dressed in unflattering maternity clothes is confined to bed. The doctor ordered that the Christmas trip home be canceled. A hospital patient has visions of medicine and loneliness, rather than sugarplums, dancing in his head. A stranded traveler glares at the TV weatherman who misinterpreted the jet stream's itinerary. Winter winds pre-

DECEMBER
18

vented his takeoff. He watches the vain attempts to clear the snow-laden runway.

God's Son was away from home that first Christmas. He was heaven's special missionary serving in a foreign land far less attractive than His own. He went away at Christmas into a small Judean town to be born in the flesh as an innocent and vulnerable baby so that we might have the opportunity to come home to God.

If you will experience a long-distance Christmas this year, remember the Son of God who lay in a meager manger. More importantly, if you are spiritually away from God the Father this Advent season, come home to Him through Jesus Christ! Mary and Joseph left Nazareth, shepherds left their hillside flocks, wise men departed from Persia. The characters of Christmas were away from home sharing Christmas with the Christ child. If you spend this holiday with Jesus, wherever you are, near or far, you'll be home for Christmas!

God's Son was away from home on Christmas!

A SON AWAY FROM HOME

My Elder Brother grew up in a home
Where love was shown on everybody's face.
He left it all above to show me His great love;
He proved His love by dying in my place.
It's hard for me to realize His great love,
It's hard to recognize He cares for me.
But He reaffirms to me that I joined His family
When I received this One who died for me.

Christmas meant a Son away from home—
His love for me so great it made Him go.
A Father's yearning, empty arms outstretched—
My Father loved enough to let Him go.

Joy Jacobs

DEAR FATHER, *thank You for the Son away from home. Please remind me that wherever I am, You are there, making that place home!*

THE GREAT EXCHANGE

For you know the grace of our Lord Jesus Christ,
that though he was rich,
yet for your sakes he became poor,
so that you through his poverty might become rich.

2 CORINTHIANS 8:9

C.s. LEWIS summarized Christmas and Christianity in one sentence: "The Son of God became a man to enable men to become sons of God" (Mere *Christianity*, p. 154). So many people strive for equality in giving gifts at Christmas. The first Christmas had no such equality. The "great exchange" occurred when God sent the pure for the impure, the Divine for the human, the Prince for the pauper. No one who looks into Bethlehem's manger will see parity. What God gave at Christmas can never be equaled through the gift giving of those who receive the priceless treasure of His Son!

The Heavenly Father was not hunting for a bargain, He was not counting pennies, and He was not shopping with coupons. He emptied heaven's bank with the expenditure of His beloved Son. The market value of His gift far exceeded the market value of any other possible present that could have been wrapped up and sent to earth. This trade was unthinkable, unjustifiable, indeed, preposterous except for the indisputable fact that God loves His creation.

DECEMBER
19

He was not interested in reciprocity; He was passionately committed to redemption. Parents of little children do not calculate their Christmas giving by what they predict their children are wrapping up for Mommy and

Daddy under the Christmas tree. The Heavenly Father has lavished upon His children a gift which is unparalleled in time and eternity. He has executed the great exchange.

The Word of God refers to this *great exchange* with a number of analogies and explanations. The New Testament has the reality of this exchange sprinkled throughout its pages. Jesus declared, "I am the good shepherd. The good shepherd lays down his life for the sheep" (John 10:11). This is a paradox, for the shepherd raises sheep for his profit, and often the sheep are sacrificed so that the shepherd may accrue gain. The roles are reversed with Jesus Christ, for the Good Shepherd sacrifices Himself for the sheep. Paul incorporated a financial reference into one of his letters to the Corinthian congregation: "For you know the grace of our Lord Jesus Christ, that though he was rich, yet for your sakes he became poor, so that you through his poverty might become rich" (2 Corinthians 8:9). Again, the apostle highlights the trade-off between two contrasting levels of wealth, the rich one becomes impoverished so that the poverty-stricken can become affluent. Peter includes a judicial assessment regarding the great exchange: "For Christ died for sins once for all, the righteous for the unrighteous, to bring you to God" (1 Peter 3:18). The righteous One, the just One, is substituted for the unrighteous, unjust one. It seems inequitable but it is the precise decision that heaven made for earth's sinners. It

He took what we deserved, so that we might have what He deserved!

appears to be unethical, but the ethics of unconditional love demand it! One of the harshest metaphors of the great exchange is offered in Galatians 3:13: "Christ redeemed us from the curse of the law by becoming a curse for us, for it is written: 'Cursed is everyone who is hung on a tree.' " The blessings of Christmas can be traced back to the cradle of Christ which was covered by the shadow of the cross. This baby had been born to die for the lost men and women of the world.

As you reflect upon God's benevolence at Bethlehem, be sure to take advantage of its benefits. He has demonstrated His willingness to purchase your salvation, your healing, your renewal via the transaction of His Son, whose birthday we cherish at Christmas!

GOOD CHRISTIAN MEN, REJOICE

Good Christian men, rejoice,
With heart and soul and voice;
Now ye hear of endless bliss:
Jesus Christ was born for this!
He hath oped the heavenly door,
And man is blessed evermore.
Christ was born for this!
Christ was born for this!

John M. Neale

DEAR FATHER, I do not understand the generosity of Your love. However, I freely accept the fact that Jesus emptied Himself that my life might be full of Your blessings. May You open doors so that I can express my gratitude for Your priceless gift.

A CARDIAC CHRISTMAS

"Here I am! I stand at the door and knock.
If anyone hears my voice and opens the door,
I will come in and eat with him, and he with me."

REVELATION 3:20

*O*NE of the villains of the Christmas story is the infamous inn-keeper, the man who had no room for Jesus. As we reflect on his cal-loused actions, we are quick to criticize and condemn. However, we face the innkeeper's choice every Christmas season. Will Christ be given room in our lives this Christmas? Even in the church at Christmas we seem to hear so many say, "My rooms are full, the calendar is so crowded, there are so many other things I have to do." Interpreted, "I have no vacancy for Christ!" How many rooms of your heart will Christ occupy this Christmas?

What is the heart according to the Word of God? In this day and age of heart attacks and heart specialists and heart problems, the words car-diovascular, cardiologist and cardiogram are used frequently. Each of these words comes from the Greek word *kardia* meaning heart. The English expressions usually refer to a physical organ which is critical for the existence of man. The biblical word *kardia* refers to a much more sophisticated and complex part of man.

Revelation 3:20 portrays Christ knocking at the door of the heart! Heart, in God's Word, refers to the main terminal of man's emotional,

DECEMBER
20

intellectual and spiritual life. Simply defined, the heart is the control center of the inner man. It is a part of God's gift. Man has the privilege of giving his heart back to God, but it is a free choice. Just like the innkeeper, you see, we have a choice as to who will occupy our rooms this Christmas!

When Jesus Christ occupies your heart it becomes a holy place, a sacred place, a divine place. There is always a difference when He steps over the threshold of a human heart. If you have Him in residence, rejoice! If you haven't invited Him in, there is no better time than this very moment!

My heart is designed to be Christ's home!

THOU DIDST LEAVE THY THRONE

Thou didst leave Thy throne and Thy kingly crown
When Thou camest to earth for me,
But in Bethlehem's home there was found no room
For Thy holy nativity.

Heaven's arches rang when the angels sang
Proclaiming Thy royal decree;
But in lowly birth didst Thou come to earth,
And in great humility.

The foxes found rest, and the birds their nest
In the shade of the forest tree,
But Thy couch was the sod, O Thou Son of God,
In the deserts of Galilee.

Oh, come to my heart, Lord Jesus:
There is room in my heart for Thee!

Emily E.S. Elliott

DEAR LORD JESUS,
I open my heart to You this Advent season. Please make Yourself at home. And if anything is out of order, please rearrange the furniture.

CHRISTMAS
OR
Christmess

After they had heard the king, they went on their way, and the star they had seen in the east went ahead of them until it stopped over the place where the child was. When they saw the star, they were overjoyed. On coming to the house, they saw the child with his mother Mary, and they bowed down and worshiped him. Then they opened their treasures and presented him with gifts of gold and of incense and of myrrh.

MATTHEW 2:9-11

*E*VERY year it is the world's biggest birthday party! We call it Christmas, the "mass" of Christ. It prompted incredible joy during that first Christmas celebration! Mary gave us "the Magnificat," a mother's praise song for the Holy One of God whose seed had been planted in her womb. The shepherds proved that the night,shift could be very exciting. A special constellation dotted the sky which canopied over the cradle of the King that inaugural Christmas Eve. Yes, it was the birthday of a majestic monarch. A Messiah had entered into the realm of earth, born of the flesh of woman. This One was the prophets' special project, the One they had foretold, the One predicted to change the world! Nothing would ever be the same—history would be more than ever History!

DECEMBER
21

Almost two millennia have passed and what has become of the birthday of the King? A.W. Tozer made this dark appraisal of our contemporary Christmas as he protested the holiday's drift from its original intent:

> *In our mad materialism we have turned beauty into ashes, prostituted every normal emotion and made merchandise of the holiest gift the world ever*

knew. Christ came to bring peace and we celebrate His coming by making peace impossible for six weeks of each year. Not peace but tension, fatigue and irritation rule the Christmas season. (The Warfare of the Spirit, p. 60)

Dr. Thomas Holmes, with his colleagues at the University of Washington, developed the now famous "stress scale" which measures the stress that certain life events bring into our lives. Christmas received a rating of twelve, almost half the value of remodeling a home, rated at twenty-five, and almost one-third the stress of pregnancy, which was rated at forty. Christmas could now be properly termed Christmess!

The first Christmas opened up the blossoms of joy in the lives of men and women like a warm sun shining on our dogwood tree in the spring. There is a natural manifestation of beauty and fulfillment when humanity worships divinity and when the sons of Adam and the daughters of Eve are confronted with the Son of God! The first Christmas wrote new chapters of joy into the diaries of those Jewish men and women and even those Gentile Magi that had followed a unique star! You and I can leave this Christmas season with our hearts full of God's love and our lips reciting the goodness of the Eternal God.

Give one gift to Christ this Christmas:

Delight in the birth of your Savior, Jesus Christ!

Forgive someone

Let go of a habit

Begin a holy habit

Love someone who doesn't love you

Accept the circumstances you are in by faith

Bow down before Him

Worship Him

Praise Him

Adore Him!

ANGELS FROM THE REALMS OF GLORY

Shepherds, in the fields abiding,
Watching o'er your flocks by night,
God with man is now residing,
Yonder shines the infant Light:
Come and worship, Come and worship,
Worship Christ, the newborn King!

James Montgomery

DEAR FATHER, *I want to delight in the birth of Your Son and our Savior Jesus Christ. Assist me in making Christmas a celebration of praise and tribute to the One whose coming transformed my world and changed my life.*

The Majesty of the Manger

This will be a sign to you:
You will find the baby wrapped in cloths and lying in a manger.

LUKE 2:12

*T*HE natal star . . . It hung suspended in the heavens above the cradle of the Christ child. This constellation was part of God's decorating of the Christmas sky that heralded the Deliverer. Its brightness guided Medo-Persian Magi to His side, beginning the gift giving we so lavishly pursue.

Bethlehem . . . It was a small town in southern Palestine. Its population hovered around 2,000. No one would have guessed that a town so insignificant among the urban centers of that time would be the predicted site of the Messiah's birth. However, it was the city of David, and seven centuries before the prophet Micah had foretold that it was the Heavenly Father's choice for the birthplace of Jesus.

DECEMBER
22

The angel's serenade . . . I remember the birth of my youngest son Marc. We left Faye in the operating room after she had delivered, and I sang to Marc as we went to another floor to get cleaned up. Baby Jesus' first night found the air sprinkled first with an angel's solo and then a full angelic choir. Despite the earthly arrangements, the angels arrived to triumphantly announce that this new arrival was divine; He was a peace child!

Mary and Joseph . . . We may belittle the dignity of Jesus' parents. Yet their ethics were of such high caliber that God expected the right response to a very difficult assignment. Mary was favored, a woman after God's heart who qualified to be the mother of God's Son. The Holy Spirit planted the seed and Mary's womb expanded with the Holy One of God! She accepted the role that would transform the teenager from Nazareth into the most honored lady of the New Testament era! And the carpenter, also from Nazareth, was God's choice to be the earthly father of Jesus. Joseph was the earthly model for and the caretaker of history's most celebrated newborn!

The Messiah in the manger . . . He was tiny, but in that little bundle of humanity was the essence of divinity. The Father had sent Him from heaven's throne, and He arrived to take on sins of the world. Perhaps the circumstances were humble, but the child was holy. Perhaps the couple was poor, but the hands of this child created the world. The message of the manger is simply this: The grace of God has come to heal the cancer of sin! In a tiny town, in a tiny manger, in a tiny baby resides all that we ever need.

Listen to the message of the manger.

THE MAGNIFICENCE OF THE HUMBLE BIRTH

Was it so humble, the birth of our King?
Should we tone it down, or should we sing?
Yes, Jesus came in infant form,
Wrapped in garment torn and worn;
Shepherds witnessed the newborn child,
Touched rough hands to the countenance mild;

A city small, Bethlehem by name,
Seems so trite, seems a shame;
A castle would have been so grand,
But stable rude with animal band;
What cradle could befit "the Good,"
A manger plain of splintered wood;
And parents of royal line and stock,
Mary, Joseph, oh what a mock.

Magnificent! Look again at the Savior's story
Even in birth surrounded by Glory.

Herald angels dawned the sky,
And proclaimed the news, Salvation nigh;
His own star of birth, with incomparable gloss,
That light a crescendo, would lead to the cross;
The person, could it greater be,
But God Himself, the Creator He;
Bethlehem, the setting of the manger bed,
How unique, a city of prophetic thread;
The Babe, not such the very start,
Did such purity adorn a heart;
The date of birth, the time of things supernal,
That date would be hallowed, continually, eternal.

Kings of kings, Lord of lords,
A royal birth God did afford.

DEAR LORD, in the Christmas story You have taught me to look beyond the obvious to the actual. May I look for the majestic even in the mundane of this world. Equip me to be sensitive to Your holy work which is often camouflaged by the details of daily living.

Two Senior Citizens

*Sovereign Lord, as you have promised, you now dismiss your servant in peace.
For my eyes have seen your salvation, which you have prepared in the sight of all people,
a light for revelation to the Gentiles and for glory to your people Israel.*

LUKE 2:29-32

*T*wo senior citizens, Simeon and Anna, are woven into the fabric of the Christmas story. Luke's account is complimentary to both of them.

Simeon is described as righteous and devout, one who maintained an optimistic outlook for his people and nation. The Holy Spirit was moving through his life, and the longevity of his earthly tenure was determined by the moment he saw the Lord's Christ.

Forty days had now passed since baby Jesus had drawn his first breath. It was now the time for Mary and Joseph to take their male child to the temple to be dedicated to God. The Spirit had alerted the elderly saint to his meeting with the divine. He was in the temple as Mary and Joseph fulfilled their duty as obedient parents of a Jewish boy.

Simeon swept the child up in his arms and at that moment, determined hope received its reward. What a special memory, the elderly saint holding up the tiny baby. He was faithful to believe that the prophets were credible and their prophecies, though incredible, would come to pass.

Simeon's response was a song, the "Nunc Dimittis," so named for the Latin rendering of the words "You now dismiss." Even though his eyes had

DECEMBER

23

witnessed the sight which signified his impending death, he was rejoicing! Simeon had the "long view" of life, a view which stretched into eternity.

Luke tells us that Anna was a relentless worshiper. She frequented the temple day and night and devoted herself to prayer and fasting (2:37). The fact that she was widowed after only seven years of marriage did not steal the joy of her faith. Now a widow for longer than most people live, she merges with the Messiah.

This dear lady came up to the couple with their special baby and gave thanks to God, announcing to all that God had sent the long-expected Deliverer.

When you worship Him, He will come to you!

No matter how young or old you are, you can be used as an instrument for the Lord. Keep worshiping, keep looking, keep holding on! You may have an appointment with the Savior!

ALL GLORY, LAUD AND HONOR

The company of angels
Are praising Thee on high,
And mortal men and all things
Created make reply.
The people of the Hebrews
With palms before Thee went;
Our praise and prayer and anthems
Before Thee we present.

Theodulph of Orleans

DEAR FATHER, *May I meet You in worship this Christmas! Give me a second wind when my faith is in respiratory failure. Please give me the "long view" of life, a view that stretches beyond the present moments of frustration to future moments of fulfilled faith.*

HE Came to us

Here is a trustworthy saying that deserves full acceptance:
Christ Jesus came into the world to save sinners.

1 TIMOTHY 1:15

CHRISTMAS can be regarded as the humbling of God's Son. God came to us through Jesus, the Creator of all things lying in a cradle. Paul wrote about this humbling in Philippians 2:5-8:

> *Your attitude should be the same as that of Christ Jesus: Who, being in very nature God, did not consider equality with God something to be grasped, but made himself nothing, taking the very nature of a servant, being made in human likeness. And being found in appearance as a man, he humbled himself and became obedient to death—even death on a cross!*

C.S. Lewis framed the humanity of God's Son in these terms:

> *The Second Person in God, became human Himself: was born into the world as an actual man—a real man of a particular height, with hair of a particular color, speaking a particular language, weighing so many stone. The Eternal Being, who knows everything and who created the whole universe, became not only a man but (before that) a baby, before that a fetus inside a Woman's body. If you want to get the hang of it, think how you would like to become a slug or a crab.* (Mere Christianity, p. 155)

DECEMBER
24

When I was growing up in a small Wesleyan Methodist church in central Pennsylvania, our pastors used object lessons to communicate the message of the gospel. The visual might be a clock, a flower, a chair or any number of physical objects. Jesus became God's living object lesson, the personification of the message of salvation. The Heavenly Father came to us through a little baby in Bethlehem. The Son of God became a human child, accessible, approachable, adorable. We did not come to Him, but He came to us!

This One who placed the stars and the planets into space came to us as the most helpless and dependent of all creatures. He came as a human baby! Humanity must not miss this message of love which was cradled that first Christmas. Kierkegaard asserted that "it is only in love that the unequal can be made equal." Jesus Christ humbled Himself so that every sinner could become a saint, every orphan a family member, every prisoner of hell a resident of heaven! His humility allows everyone who believes in His purpose, His power, His pardon to be lifted up.

God was not willing that any should perish so He sent His Son to pay the redemption price. The angel reported to the shepherds: "Today in the town of David a Savior has been born to you; he is Christ the Lord" (Luke 2:11). The sinner did not stretch himself to meet the Savior, the Savior stretched Himself to meet the sinner. "We love because he first loved us" (1 John 4:19).

He came and He's coming again!

We remember at Christmas the Heavenly Father's overture to the inhabitants of earth. Look into the manger and your eyes will view the Messiah. He is the Deliverer. He came to us, He came for us!

He came to us, and He will come again! Have you made room in your heart for Him? If you have, you experienced the sweet and powerful love of God. If you have not known His company, this promise is for you: "Here I am! I stand at the door and knock. If anyone hears my voice and opens the door, I will come in and eat with him, and he with me" (Revelation 3:20).

HE CAME TO US

He was First Light, He was First Love,
Not from the earth, The Father sent Him from above;
We all deserved the ruin and disgrace,
He came to us and brought us grace.

He was The Truth, He was The Way,
The Incarnation, It began a brand New Day;
Our dreams all gone, Our hopes had ceased,
He came to us and brought us peace.

He was The Lamb, He was The Price,
The Son of God, became the bleeding sacrifice,
We were so lost, so all alone,
He came to us and brought us home.

DEAR HEAVENLY FATHER,
I am amazed and inspired by the personification of Your love in Bethlehem's bed. The gift of Jesus is so unmerited and yet so necessary for my salvation. I praise Him for coming.

A Second Advent

"Men of Galilee," they said, "why do you stand here looking into the sky?
This same Jesus, who has been taken from you into heaven,
will come back in the same way you have seen him go into heaven."
Then they returned to Jerusalem from the hill called the Mount of Olives,
a Sabbath day's walk from the city.

ACTS 1:11-12

Virtually every Christian church in America will sing "Joy to the world, the Lord is come" this holiday season. Christmas is testimony to this fact: God fulfills His promises. God promised a Savior and it came to pass in the fullness of time! God's sense of timing is more precise than a gold Swiss watch. There was a special moment in history when conditions were ripe for His first Advent!

The night of Jesus' birth found the world under the rule of the Roman Empire. Due to the military strength of this giant enterprise, this resulted in the *Pax Romana*, a time of incredible peace in the world. A network of roadways had been constructed over the ancient world allowing for free passage and travel. The Greek language was spoken almost universally due to the influence of Alexander the Great and his dream to Hellenize the world. Caesar Augustus himself, whose reign extended more than four decades, was very religious and favored tolerance for other faiths and their expression! History was now ripe for the sending of God's Deliverer. He took residence in Mary's virgin womb.

DECEMBER
25

But when Jesus Christ came, most of the world was unaware and really not expecting Him. Yes, a long recital of prophets had heralded His coming. Yes, God had been faithful to carry out His predictions and promises in times past. However, the wait had stretched into centuries and no prophet had spoken for over 400 years. The Jewish people had been passed from one empire to another like a piece of luggage. The prophecies were dusty and hopes had evaporated. Humanity was caught off guard.

Yet there were a few devout people like Simeon and Anna in the vicinity of the temple who looked with elevated expectation for this great Redeemer. But they were a minority so not many noticed when He came as a tiny child in a crude cradle.

On this Christmas morning we can believe that He lived and moved among us. His teaching was unmatched, His miracles were many and His death was tragic and inevitable. But God raised Him up, and He stood on the Mountain of Olives and ascended into Heaven.

Will the world be caught flat-footed when He comes again? The New Testament mentions this Second Advent, this subsequent coming, over 300 times. He is coming again! God has not misplaced His date book. Are you ready for His return, which the New Testament compares to the strike of lightning or a thief in the night? Ask Him to forgive your sins and make your heart His home. If you have already done that, make sure your affections are set on Him and you are making the invisible Christ visible.

Most of the world was abysmally unprepared for His first Advent! You

Joy to the world, the Lord is coming!

and I can be among those who have our tickets stamped and our luggage packed when He makes His encore visit.

THOU DIDST LEAVE THY THRONE

When the heavens shall ring and the angels sing
At Thy coming to victory,
Let Thy voice call me home, saying,
"Yet there is room, There is room at My side for thee."
And my heart shall rejoice, Lord Jesus,
When Thou comest and callest for me.

Emily E.S. Elliott

DEAR HEAVENLY FATHER,
You are Lord of time and eternity. You, and only You, know the appointed moment of Jesus' return. Enable me to stay awake. I fervently pray that I may joyfully share in the glorious call that Jesus will extend to His Church.